THE STORY BEHIND

PLASTIC

Christin Ditchfield

Heinemann Library
Chicago, Illinois

www.heinemannraintree.com
Visit our website to find out
more information about
Heinemann-Raintree books.

To order:
☎ Phone 888-454-2279
💻 Visit www.heinemannraintree.com
to browse our catalog and order online.

© 2012 Heinemann Library
an imprint of Capstone Global Library, LLC
Chicago, Illinois

Edited by Megan Cotugno and Diyan Leake
Designed by Philippa Jenkins
Original illustrations © Capstone Global
    Library Ltd (2011)
Illustrated by Philippa Jenkins
Picture research by Hannah Taylor and Mica Brancic
Originated by Capstone Global Library Ltd
Printed and bound in China by CTPS

15 14 13 12 11
10 9 8 7 6 5 4 3 2 1

Library of Congress Cataloging-in-Publication Data
Ditchfield, Christin.
  The story behind plastic / Christin Ditchfield.
    p. cm.—(True stories)
  Includes bibliographical references and indexes.
  ISBN 978-1-4329-5441-3 (hc)
  1. Plastics—Juvenile literature. I. Title.
  TP1125.D58 2012
  668.4—dc22   2010044356

Acknowledgments
We would like to thank the following for permission
to reproduce photographs: Alamy p. **20** (© Marcelo
Rudini); Corbis pp. **16** (Peter Ginter), **23** (Reuters/Luke
MacGregor); Getty Images pp. **5** (Science & Society
Picture Library), **6** (Three Lions), **24** (Bloomberg/ Chip
Chipman); istockphoto pp. **18** (© Skip O Donnell), **21**
(© Miguel Malo); NASA p. **12**; Science Photo Library
p. **27** (Paul Rapson); Shutterstock pp. **iii** (© Jiri Hera), **4**
(© Seregam), **7** (© Arena Creative), **8** (© nadi555), **9**
(© Irina Silayeva), **10** (© vladm), **14** (© Elena Schweitzer),
15 (© indianstockimages), **19** (© Maridav), **11** (© Maxim
Ahner), **13** (© Mircea Bezergheanu), **22** (© Perov Stanislav),
25 (© Konstantin Yolshin), **26** (© Stéphane Bidouze).

Cover photograph of drinking straws reproduced with
permission of istockphoto (Rob Eyers.)

We would like to thank Ann Fullick for her invaluable help
in the preparation of this book.

Every effort has been made to contact copyright holders of
material reproduced in this book. Any omissions will be
rectified in subsequent printings if notice is given to the
publisher.

Disclaimer
All the Internet addresses (URLs) given in this book were
valid at the time of going to press. However, due to the
dynamic nature of the Internet, some addresses may have
changed, or sites may have changed or ceased to exist since
publication. While the author and publisher regret any
inconvenience this may cause readers, no responsibility for
any such changes can be accepted by either the author or
the publisher.

Contents

■ **An Amazing Invention** 4

■ **The History of Plastic** 6

■ **So Many Kinds of Plastic, So Many Uses** 10

■ **Why Plastics Are Special** ... 14

■ **What Plastics Are Made Of** .. 16

■ **How Plastics Are Made** 20

■ **Recycling Plastic** 22

■ **The Future of Plastic** 26

■ *Timeline* 28

■ *Glossary* 30

■ *Find Out More* 31

■ *Index* 32

Some words are shown in bold, **like this**. You can find out what they mean by looking in the glossary on page 30.

An Amazing Invention

▲ All these things are made of plastic.

Plastic—it's everywhere! Put this book down and look around you. You'll probably see at least 15 things made of plastic: a pen, your backpack, jacket, shoes, a drink cup or water bottle, a snack wrapper, a CD or DVD, a ball, a bookshelf, markers, and a whiteboard.

Plastic is a material made of plants, wood fibers, or oil. With heat and pressure, it can be molded into all kinds of shapes and used to make all kinds of objects—from toys, to traffic lights, to bullet-proof vests. Plastic has changed the way we live.

The Great International Exhibition

At the 1862 Great International Exhibition in London, an Englishman named Alexander Parkes introduced a new product he called Parkesine. It was the first plastic that anyone had made. Parkes explained that this hard, solid substance became soft and flexible when it was heated. It could be shaped into tools and other useful objects. It could also be used to coat other objects and make them water-**resistant**.

▼ British chemist and inventor Alexander Parkes created the first human-made plastic.

Alexander Parkes (1813–1890)

Alexander Parkes was born in Birmingham, England, in 1813. He won a bronze medal at the 1862 Great International Exhibition for his invention of Parkesine. He had originally been trying to find a replacement for ivory (the material that elephant tusks are made of). Parkes loved inventing new things and had **patents** (rights) on many of his inventions. He also fathered 20 children!

The History of Plastic

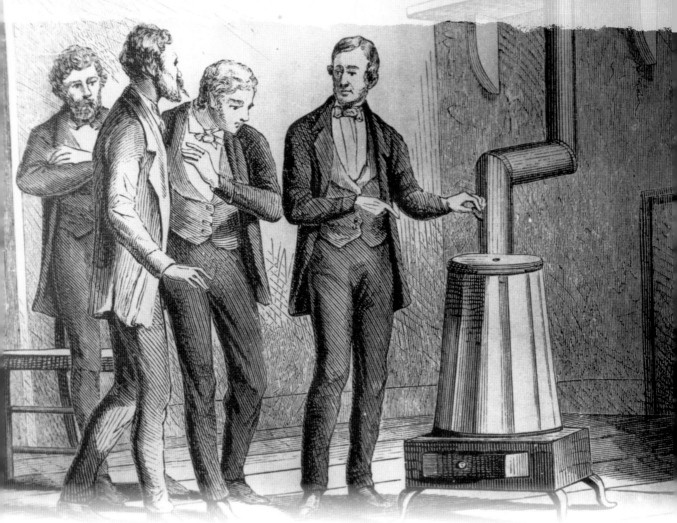

▲ The Goodyear Tire and Rubber Company was named in honor of Charles Goodyear and the work that he did to improve the qualities of natural rubber.

Rubber is a natural plastic. It comes from the milky sap of rubber trees. In 1839, U.S. inventor Charles Goodyear conducted experiments with rubber. He wanted to see if he could improve its qualities or **characteristics**. Natural rubber is sticky. It gets soft and gooey in the heat. It gets hard and snaps or breaks in the cold.

Goodyear discovered that heating rubber with a **chemical** (substance) called sulphur changed the texture. It made the rubber strong, elastic (stretchy), and waterproof. Now this rubber could be used for things like tires, shoe soles, garden hoses, and even ice hockey pucks!

More natural plastics

With Goodyear's **vulcanization** process, scientists created a hard, black rubber called vulcanite or ebonite. It was used to make combs and brushes, buttons, jewelry, and eventually bowling balls. In 1839, a German scientist named Eduard Simon discovered an oily, jelly-like plastic that came from the Turkish sweet gum tree. He called it **polystyrene**. Today a chemical form of polystyrene is used to make food and drink containers, packaging materials, **disposable** razors, and CD jewel cases.

In 1856, U.S. inventors Alfred Critchlow and Samuel Peck found that the female lac bug (a tiny insect found in the forests of India and Thailand) oozes a sticky liquid called resin. When the resin is dissolved in alcohol, it creates a clear liquid coating that hardens and protects the surfaces of wood and other substances. They called this coating shellac.

◄ Different kinds of plastic are used to make disposable eating utensils and food and drink containers.

▲ Film is made from a kind of plastic called celluloid.

A winning discovery

In 1863, a United States inventor named John Wesley Hyatt read about a contest offering $10,000 to anyone who could come up with a new material for making billiard balls. At the time, billiard balls were made of ivory, which comes from elephant tusks. Ivory was getting too expensive and too difficult to find.

Hyatt won the contest with his invention of celluloid, a mixture of wood fibers and a waxy substance called camphor. Celluloid turned out to be a much more important discovery than Hyatt first realized. This new plastic was soon used for taking photographs and making movies.

In the spotlight

In the 1800s, George Eastman perfected celluloid film. This flexible film led to the development of Thomas Edison's motion picture camera in 1891.

The age of plastics

Dr. Leo Hendrick Baekeland (1863–1944) was a U.S. **chemistry** professor who wanted to improve on the inventions of ebonite, shellac, and celluloid. In 1909, he used chemicals called phenol and formaldehyde to create the world's first truly **synthetic** (human-made) plastic. It was called Bakelite. Unlike the other plastics, Bakelite did not come from any substance found in nature. It was an entirely new chemical creation.

Bakelite was so much stronger and longer-lasting than other plastics. It was also much cheaper to make and sell. Factories all over the world began producing this new plastic. It was used for everything from clocks, radios, telephones, and jewelry, to children's toys, electric guitars, and the first machine guns used in World War I (1914–1918).

▼ Telephones made from Bakelite were once very popular for ordinary, everyday use. Today they are valuable collectors' items or antiques.

So Many Kinds of Plastic, So Many Uses

▲ Many medical supplies are made of disposable plastics.

In the 1920s and 1930s, many new kinds of plastic were developed and put to use. Over time, scientists working for chemical companies figured out new ways to use and improve these plastics.

Formica (a hard, strong plastic with a shiny surface) became a popular material for kitchen countertops. PVC (polyvinyl chloride) was used to make pipes for plumbing, gutters, shower curtains, and flooring. Melamine cups, bowls, and plates didn't break if you dropped them. Clear plastic Saran wrap covered foods and kept them from spoiling. Vinyl could be used to make anything from window frames and medical supplies, to articles of clothing.

Polyester was another plastic that could be used to make wrinkle-free, stain-resistant clothing. Scientists found that acrylic could imitate fabrics such as wool. It could also be used to create certain kinds of paint and a type of clear, shatter-resistant "glass."

The invention of nylon

Wallace Hume Carothers (1896–1937) worked for the DuPont Chemical Corporation in the United States. While he was trying to find substitutes for rubber, he invented nylon and neoprene. Nylon is a plastic that can be drawn out into long, thin fibers, like silk. It is lightweight, strong, and long-lasting. Manufacturers use nylon to make toothbrush bristles, rope, tents, parachutes, luggage, and pantyhose.

A big investment

The DuPont chemical company spent 12 years and $27 million inventing nylon, including finding ways to manufacture it and use it.

◀ Laptop covers, wetsuits for swimmers and divers, and Halloween masks are all made of neoprene. This soft, rubbery plastic is also used for wrist, elbow, knee, and ankle supports.

▲ Space exploration has been made possible in part by the invention of plastics.

New discoveries and new inventions

Sometimes it took years for teams of scientists to work out how to use a plastic that had been invented or discovered much earlier. For instance, Roy Plunkett was working at the DuPont Chemical Corporation in 1938. He created a slippery plastic coating called Teflon. It wasn't until the 1960s that manufacturers found a way to use Teflon to coat kitchen pots and pans, so that food wouldn't stick to them!

In the 1960s and 1970s, scientists explored many new chemical combinations and processes for creating and working with plastics. In the 1980s, a plastic called Kevlar (invented by American Stephanie Kwolek) was used to make bullet-proof body armor for police officers and members of the military.

Scientists also worked to develop plastics that could withstand extremely high temperatures. These new plastics were used to make parts for cars, airplanes, and spacecraft.

Other new plastics worked better for computers, cell phones, and digital music players. Some are used to make glasses and contact lenses. Some provide layers of insulation or protection for electrical wires, machines, and equipment.

Scientists all over the world are still experimenting. They are always improving or replacing old plastics with new and better plastics.

◄ In the 1800s, U.S. inventors John Jacob Bausch and Henry Lomb discovered that eyeglass frames could be made from inexpensive plastics, rather than costly metals. Today eyeglass lenses and contact lenses are also made of plastic.

Why Plastics Are Special

▲ Plastics come in many colors, shapes, and sizes.

Over the last century, plastic products have gradually replaced hundreds of products that used to be made with other materials such as paper, wood, stone, metal, glass, pottery, and leather. This is because plastics have some special qualities. They can be molded into any shape or size. They can be dyed any color—or left clear.

Plastics can be made softer, harder, or stretchier than other natural materials. They don't break as easily as glass, pottery, or bones. They don't rot or decay, so they last longer than paper or wood products. They don't rust like metal, or get moldy like leather.

Most plastics are cheap and easy to make. They are disposable. We don't have to repair plastic items that are broken. We don't need to clean plastic items that have been exposed to germs and diseases. Plastic items can be easily replaced.

Unlike water and metal, plastic does not conduct electricity. In other words, electricity cannot travel through it. So plastic works as an **insulator**, to protect people and things from damage caused by lightning or power surges.

Most importantly, plastic does not dissolve or break down in water. It doesn't react to the chemicals in soap, alcohol, gasoline, and other substances. So, plastic can be used to make containers to carry these things!

Warning!

Plastics are not always cheap. It depends on what they are made from. Plastics made from **petroleum** (oil) are becoming increasingly expensive. This is because there is only a limited supply of petroleum chemicals and they are **nonrenewable**. It is important to **recycle** and reuse these plastics.

▼ These wires are covered with a protective layer of plastic.

What Plastics Are Made Of

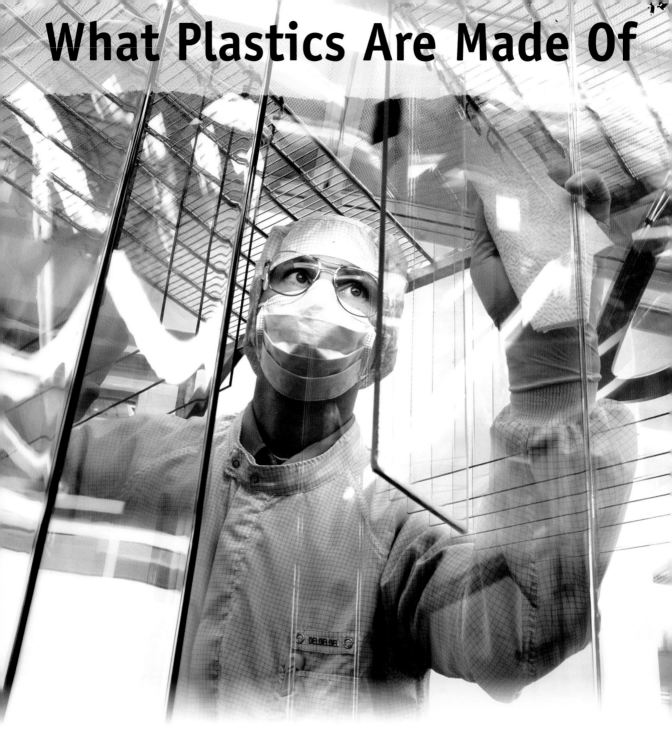

▲ This scientist is checking the quality of sheets of a plastic polymer called Makrolon. Light shines better through Makrolon than through glass.

Most of the **chemical** ingredients used to make plastic come from petroleum, although some come from plant and wood fibers. Scientists take these chemicals from nature or recreate them in a **laboratory** in order to form plastics.

All plastics are made up of groups of **hydrocarbon molecules**. These are molecules that have thousands and thousands of hydrogen **atoms** and carbon atoms. Some also have oxygen, nitrogen, chlorine, or sulfur atoms.

How plastics work

Small hydrocarbon molecules called monomers are joined together with other monomers to create large molecules called polymers. Scientists arrange these polymers in long repeating chains, ladders, rings, or branches. What makes one plastic different from another is the number of polymers it has, the type of polymers, the combination of different polymers, and the way these polymers are linked together.

What it means

In Greek, *mono* means "one" and *mer* means "part" or "unit." So a monomer has one part or unit. *Poly* means "many," so a polymer is something made of many parts or units.

▼ Plastics are made of hydrocarbons—molecules formed by hydrogen and carbon atoms joined together in groups or chains like these.

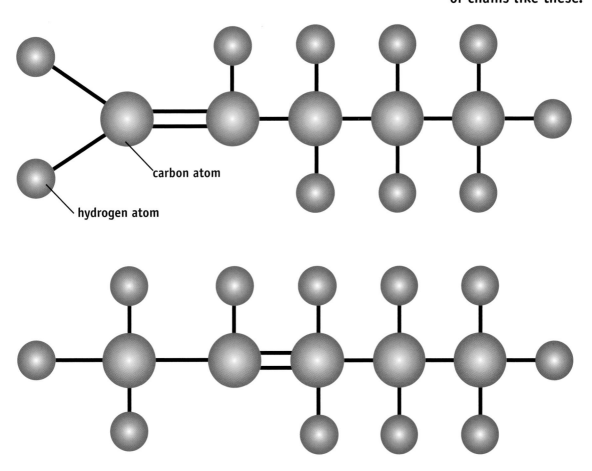

carbon atom

hydrogen atom

▲ Polyurethane is an example of a thermoset plastic. It is used to make things like car parts and skateboard wheels.

Grouping plastics

The many different kinds of plastic can be organized into groups or categories. These categories might describe the main ingredients of the plastic or the quality of the plastic. They can also describe the characteristics of the plastic and what kind of products it is used for. Most of the time, however, scientists put plastics into one of two categories: thermoset plastics and thermoplastics.

Thermoset plastics

All plastics are created by combining the chemical ingredients and heating them until they turn into a liquid. This liquid plastic is poured into molds. When the liquid cools down, it hardens and takes the shape of the molds.

Thermoset plastics can only be heated once, during the process in which they are created. Once they have cooled, they stay in the shape in which they have been made. If a thermoset plastic is exposed to heat again, it melts into a gooey chemical mess that cannot be reused.

Thermoplastics

Thermoplastics can be heated and reheated, shaped and reshaped. A thermoplastic cup, for instance, can be melted down and remade into a bowl.

▼ This hula hoop is made of polyethylene. Polyethylene is a thermoplastic. It is the most widely used plastic in the world.

How Plastics Are Made

▲ Plastic is made in large quantities in factories like this one.

Plastics are made in factories all over the world. Manufacturers (companies that make things to sell) follow special recipes or formulas to create the specific kind of plastic they want. They mix all the chemical ingredients together in giant tanks. A machine like a blender adds both heat and pressure as the mixture spins around inside. At this stage, the monomers are joining to each other to become polymers.

Manufacturers add other chemicals that will give the plastic its color or make it fire resistant or extra shiny—whatever important qualities they want the plastic to have.

The plastic that comes through this process looks like little beads or pellets. These pellets will be heated until they melt into a liquid. The liquid goes into a mold that gives the plastic its shape.

Different kinds of molds produce different kinds of shapes—from bracelets, to toys, to computer keyboards, to cups, bowls, and plates. As the plastic cools, it hardens. Sometimes a special protective coating is added to the finished product.

▼ **These plastic pellets will be melted down into liquid plastic and poured into molds of different shapes and sizes.**

21

Recycling Plastic

▲ Plastic drinking bottles can always be reused and recycled.

Today we produce and use 20 times more plastic than we did 50 years ago. About a billion tons of that plastic has just been thrown away. Other types of trash—such as food waste, yard waste, or items made of natural substances such as cotton, wool, or wood—will eventually rot. These things break down into pieces, eaten by tiny bacteria. However, most bacteria do not eat plastic! Plastic does not easily break down. It will last for hundreds, and maybe thousands, of years.

How recycling works

Since the 1990s, people all over the world have been learning to reuse and recycle plastic. Plastic bags, bottles, and other items are collected and sent to recycling plants. There, workers separate the plastics by type and category. The plastics are shredded, washed, and dried. Then machines melt the plastics back into a liquid form. They filter out any bits and pieces of trash. Once the plastic has cooled and hardened, it is shredded into pellets and sold back to plastic manufacturing companies.

Bottles and more bottles

People in the United States buy billions of plastic water bottles each year. Only three out of every ten of these bottles makes its way to a recycling plant. The rest are piled up in landfills and garbage dumps.

▼ **Many plastics can be sent to recycling plants like this one.**

23

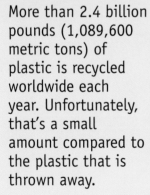

► Recycling plastic can be more difficult and more expensive than making new plastic.

Problems with recycling

The process of recycling can be expensive. It takes a lot of time and energy to sort the different kinds of plastic. They can't all be combined, even if they are the same kind of plastic, because some are different colors or have different chemical ingredients that don't mix well. There are a lot of plastics that simply can't be recycled. It is too difficult and complicated to break them down—or when they have been broken down, they can't be reused.

Things you can do

1. Refill and reuse your plastic water bottles, instead of buying new ones. When it's time to discard the bottles, make sure they go into a recycling bin.
2. Reuse plastic shopping bags or take reusable cloth bags to the store.
3. Donate used plastic toys to thrift stores, instead of throwing them away.
4. Take plastic containers to schools or craft centers, where they can be reused in creative ways.
5. Buy products that are made from recycled materials or that have very little packaging. If possible, the packaging should be made from ingredients that can be recycled.

▼ You can do your part for the environment by reusing and recycling plastic water bottles.

The Future of Plastic

▲ Plastic litter like this can build up in lakes and rivers, posing a major threat to fish, birds, and other wildlife.

Many people are becoming concerned about the amount of plastic—and the kinds of plastic—that are a part of our daily lives. This is not just because of the amount of plastic that we throw away. Some plastics have been found to contain chemicals that cause **cancer** and other diseases. These chemicals are released when the plastic is microwaved, heated, or burned at a garbage dump.

Making it work

The plastic rings that hold six-packs of soft drinks together have caused a lot of damage to the environment—especially to the fish, birds, and other animals that get caught in the plastic loops that people have thrown away. Scientists have created a new formula or recipe for this plastic, so that it is now photodegradable. This means that in sunlight, the plastic rings dissolve into powder after a few months.

Today scientists are working hard to find new ways to recycle and break down the kinds of plastics that are filling up our landfill sites. They are also trying to create new plastics that are safer and healthier for us and better for the environment.

▼ **This packaging is made of a biodegradable plastic wrapper. If it is placed in a landfill, garbage pile, or compost pile, it will eventually break down and dissolve completely.**

Timeline

(These dates are often approximations.)

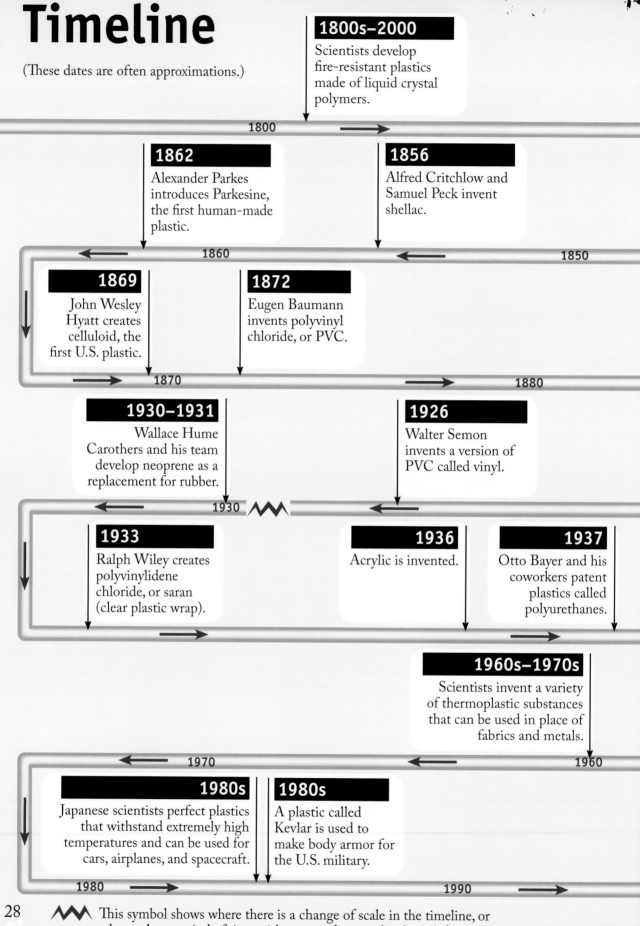

1800s–2000
Scientists develop fire-resistant plastics made of liquid crystal polymers.

1800

1862
Alexander Parkes introduces Parkesine, the first human-made plastic.

1856
Alfred Critchlow and Samuel Peck invent shellac.

1860

1850

1869
John Wesley Hyatt creates celluloid, the first U.S. plastic.

1872
Eugen Baumann invents polyvinyl chloride, or PVC.

1870

1880

1930–1931
Wallace Hume Carothers and his team develop neoprene as a replacement for rubber.

1926
Walter Semon invents a version of PVC called vinyl.

1930

1933
Ralph Wiley creates polyvinylidene chloride, or saran (clear plastic wrap).

1936
Acrylic is invented.

1937
Otto Bayer and his coworkers patent plastics called polyurethanes.

1960s–1970s
Scientists invent a variety of thermoplastic substances that can be used in place of fabrics and metals.

1970

1960

1980s
Japanese scientists perfect plastics that withstand extremely high temperatures and can be used for cars, airplanes, and spacecraft.

1980s
A plastic called Kevlar is used to make body armor for the U.S. military.

1980

1990

28   This symbol shows where there is a change of scale in the timeline, or where a long period of time with no noted events has been left out.

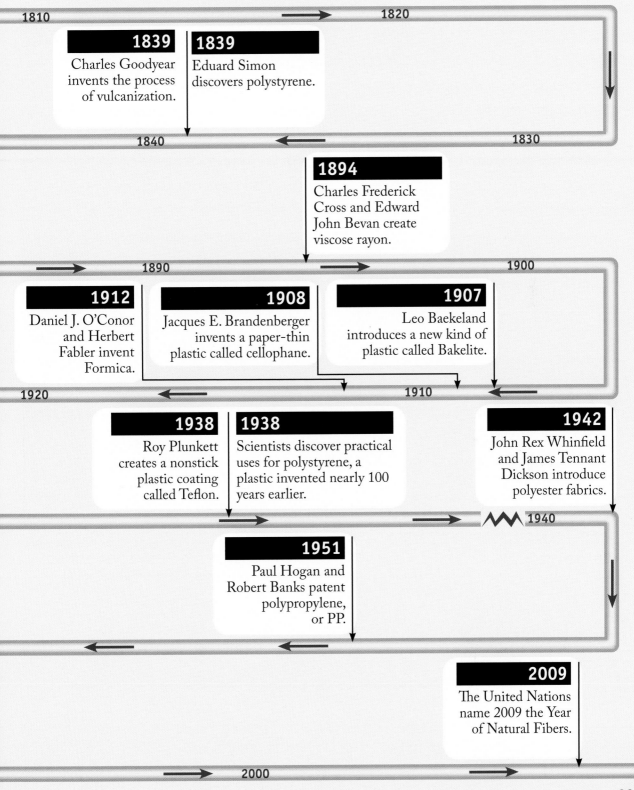

1810   1820

1839
Charles Goodyear invents the process of vulcanization.

1839
Eduard Simon discovers polystyrene.

1840   1830

1894
Charles Frederick Cross and Edward John Bevan create viscose rayon.

1890   1900

1912
Daniel J. O'Conor and Herbert Fabler invent Formica.

1908
Jacques E. Brandenberger invents a paper-thin plastic called cellophane.

1907
Leo Baekeland introduces a new kind of plastic called Bakelite.

1920   1910

1938
Roy Plunkett creates a nonstick plastic coating called Teflon.

1938
Scientists discover practical uses for polystyrene, a plastic invented nearly 100 years earlier.

1942
John Rex Whinfield and James Tennant Dickson introduce polyester fabrics.

1940

1951
Paul Hogan and Robert Banks patent polypropylene, or PP.

2009
The United Nations name 2009 the Year of Natural Fibers.

2000

Glossary

atom tiniest part of an element, a substance that cannot be made any smaller

cancer disease in which some cells grow very quickly, forming lumps that may spread through the body

characteristic feature that makes a substance special or different from others

chemical substance that can be made into other substances by changing its atoms or molecules

chemistry study of substances, what they are made of, and how they react to each other

disposable made to be thrown away after use

hydrocarbon molecule made of hydrogen and carbon atoms

insulator something that surrounds and protects an object from heat and electricity

laboratory place used for science experiments and tests

molecule tiny particle composed of one or more atoms

nonrenewable something that cannot be replaced once it runs out

patent rights to an invention for a limited period of time. The patent allows the owner to make money from an invention without competition from other companies.

petroleum an oil found under ground or under the seabed

polystyrene a plastic first found in the Turkish sweet gum tree, now produced in a chemical form

recycle use over again, sometimes in a new way

resistant keeps something (such as water) out

synthetic substance that is human-made (from chemicals), not found in nature

vulcanization treating rubber with sulfur to make it strong, elastic, and waterproof

Find Out More

Books

Blaxland, Wendy. *Bottles and Jars*. New York: Benchmark Books, 2010.

Finkelstein, Norman H. *Pastics*. New York: Benchmark Books, 2007.

Morris, Neil. *Plastics*. Mankato, MN: Amicus, 2010.

Rae, Alison. *Oil, Plastics, and Power*. Mankato, MN: Smart Apple Media, 2009.

Thomson, Ruth. *Plastics*. Mankato, MN: Smart Apple Media, 2006.

Wallace, Holly. *Plastic*. Mankato, MN: Smart Apple Media, 2007.

DVD

Baker, Tom. *Inventions that Changed Our Lives: Plastic Planet*. San Fancisco: Cerebellum Corporation, 2007.

Websites

http://www.sea.edu/plastics/index.htm
The Sea Education Association (SEA) studies the effects of plastic debris fields on the environment of the world's oceans.

http://www.americanchemistry.com/s_plastics/doc.asp?CID=1102&DID=4665
This website of the American Chemistry Council provides a history of the development of plastics. The American Chemistry Council represents companies involved in the use of chemicals and plastics.

http://www.epa.gov/kids/index.htm
Join the club! You'll find all kinds of fun facts, quizzes, games, and activities for kids on the United States Environmental Protection Agency's website.

http://www.sciencenewsforkids.org/articles/20081008/Note3.asp
This website has all the latest science news, including an article on the discovery of "Plastic-Munching Microbes" that may help us recycle water bottles and other plastics in the future.

Index

acrylic 11
atoms 17

Bakelite 9
biodegradable materials
    22, 23, 27

camera film 8
cancer 26
celluloid 8
characteristics of
    plastics 14–15
color 14, 20

disposable products 7,
    10, 14

ebonite 7
environmental damage
    26–27

formaldehyde 9
formica 10
fructose 27

Goodyear, Charles 6

history of plastics 5–9
hydrocarbons 17

ingredients of plastics 4,
    15, 16–17, 27
insulator 15

Kevlar 13

Makrolon 16
manufacturing plastics
    20–21
melamine 10
molecules 17
monomers 17, 20
molded 4, 14, 18, 21

neoprene 11
nylon 11

Parkes, Alexander 5
Parkesine 5
petroleum (oil) 15, 16
phenol 9
photodegradable plastic
    27
polyester 11
polyethylene 19
polymers 16, 17, 20
polystyrene 7
polyurethane 18
PVC (polyvinyl
    chloride) 10

recycling and reusing
    15, 22–25
resin 7
rubber 6

saran 10

shellac 7
space exploration 12

Teflon 12
thermoplastics 19
thermoset plastics
    18–19

uses of plastics 10–13

vinyl 10
vulcanite 7
vulcanization 6, 7

water bottles 22, 23, 25
water-resistance 5